# PLANES
## on the Move

**Willow Clark**

**PowerKiDS**
press™

New York

*To Dan, for our "buddy time" in the Santiago airport*

Published in 2010 by The Rosen Publishing Group, Inc.
29 East 21st Street, New York, NY 10010

First Edition

Editor: Nicole Pristash
Book Design: Kate Laczynski
Photo Researcher: Jessica Gerweck

Photo Credits: Cover, p. 1 Check Six/Getty Images; p. 4 Courtesy of the Department of Defense; p. 6 Time & Life Pictures/Getty Images; pp. 8, 14–15 Shutterstock.com; p. 10 Tim Matsui/Getty Images; p. 12 © www.istockphoto.com/brytta; p. 16 © www.istockphoto.com/Theo Fitzhugh; p. 18 © U.S. Air Force/agefotostock; p. 20 © 2009 Associated Press/AP Images.

Library of Congress Cataloging-in-Publication Data

Clark, Willow.
  Planes on the move / Willow Clark. — 1st ed.
      p. cm. — (Transportation station)
  Includes index.
  ISBN 978-1-4358-9332-0 (library binding) — ISBN 978-1-4358-9752-6 (pbk.) — ISBN 978-1-4358-9753-3 (6-pack)
  1. Aeronautics—Juvenile literature. 2. Airplanes—Juvenile literature. I. Title.
  TL547.C465 2010
  629.133'34—dc22
                                        2009022619

Manufactured in the United States of America

CPSIA Compliance Information: Batch #WW10PK: For Further Information contact Rosen Publishing, New York, New York at 1-800-237-9932

# Contents

**4**

*This is an F-16 Fighting Falcon. F-16s are some of the most commonly used planes in the U.S. Air Force.*

# High in the Sky

Have you ever flown in an airplane? If so, you have seen how high planes can fly. Planes fly above trees and higher than birds. They can even fly higher than clouds! Planes are fast, and because they fly over mountains and oceans, they are a great way to travel.

Planes are not used only by travelers flying on **commercial** airlines, though. Militaries use planes to carry soldiers and **cargo**. Businesses use planes to move their goods from place to place. Airplanes help people get things done. They are some of the most interesting vehicles in the world.

This picture shows Orville (lying on plane) and Wilbur
(standing) Wright making one of the first piloted, powered,
and controlled airplane flights.

6

# Orville and Wilbur Get It Right

By the beginning of the twentieth century, flying machines, such as hot-air balloons and **gliders**, had been invented. However, two brothers, Orville and Wilbur Wright, wanted to make a better flying machine. They studied how birds fly, along with past inventions. On December 17, 1903, the brothers made the first **piloted**, powered, and controlled airplane flight.

Planes have changed a lot since then. The Wright brothers' first flight traveled 120 feet (37 m), and it lasted 12 seconds. Today, it is possible to fly 18.5 hours nonstop from New York City to Singapore, which is a distance of 9,531 miles (15,339 km)!

Above the wing, fast-moving air creates low pressure.

Under the wing, slow-moving air creates high pressure. The high pressure causes lift.

The labels in the picture show how air pressure and wind speed cause lift, making flight possible.

# How Planes Fly

An airplane's wings are curved on top, which creates fast-moving air and low **pressure** above the wings. The bottoms of the wings are flat, which creates slow-moving air and high pressure under the wings. The high pressure pushes the plane up, causing lift. The airplane's engine supplies thrust, or forward movement. To create flight, lift and thrust work against drag and **gravity**, the forces that push the plane backward and down.

Today's planes are made of metal, such as aluminum and titanium, and **composite materials**. These materials are light, so they allow the plane to get off the ground easily.

The shape of Concorde's famous nose was pointed so that there was less air resistance. The shape also helped the pilot see out of the window easily.

10

# Passenger Planes

If you have flown on a plane while taking a trip, then you have flown on a **passenger** plane. Passenger planes take people all over the world. Some are small and seat around 30 people. Large planes, such as a Boeing 777, can seat more than 350 people.

One passenger plane stands out from the rest. The Concorde was a **supersonic** passenger jet that flew passengers between 1976 and 2003. It flew twice as fast as other planes. Generally, a flight from London to New York takes 8 hours. Flying at 1,330 miles per hour (2,140 km/h), a Concorde made the trip in 3.5 hours!

*Seaplanes, such as this one, are often used along the coast and around the lakes of Alaska. Because Alaska is so mountainous, seaplanes allow people to travel the area easily.*

# On the Water

Most passenger planes land on and take off from the ground. However, some planes land on and take off from the water! These planes are called seaplanes. One type of seaplane is the floatplane. A floatplane looks like other planes except that it has floats where the wheels would generally be. Floats are special parts that allow the plane to move along the top of the water as it takes off and lands.

Seaplanes are often used in places where there are islands surrounded by a lot of water. These small planes make it easy for people to travel from one island to another.

# INFORMATION STATION

1. Artist Leonardo da Vinci made drawings of his ideas about flight in the 1480s, although he never tried to build a flying machine.

2. Brothers Joseph and Jacques Montgolfier invented the hot-air balloon in 1783. The balloon's first passengers were a sheep, a rooster, and a duck.

3. A Boeing 777 can fly at a height of 43,100 feet (13,137 m), which is a little over 8 miles (13 km)!

4. Airplanes generally leave a smoke trail behind them. However, the F-22A Raptor leaves less smoke. This makes it hard for the enemies to know the plane was there.

**5** The first person to fly solo and nonstop across the Atlantic Ocean was Charles Lindbergh in 1927.

**6** When a plane hits supersonic speed, people on the ground hear a loud sound called a sonic boom.

**7** In 1928, Amelia Earhart became the first woman to fly across the Atlantic Ocean as a passenger. In 1932, she became the first woman pilot to fly solo across it.

*This F-22A Raptor has a vapor cloud around it. Vapor, a liquid that has turned into a gas, forms on planes when they travel at or near the speed of sound.*

# Safety and Stealth

Planes have been used by the world's militaries since the early 1900s. Military planes are used to carry soldiers and cargo. They also carry **weapons**, such as guns, **missiles**, and bombs. These weapons are used to fight enemies and to keep soldiers safe from harm.

The F-22A Raptor is one of the newest fighting planes in the U.S. military. The Raptor is a stealth plane. A stealth plane is made in a way that makes it hard for **radar** to find it until it is very close. The Raptor is fast. It can travel over 1,300 miles per hour (2,092 km/h)!

*The MQ-1 Predator, shown here, is controlled by a crew from miles (km) away. If the plane is hit by an enemy, there is no one in the plane who could get hurt.*

# Planes Without Pilots

Did you know that there are military planes that can fly without pilots? The MQ-1 Predator is an unmanned aerial vehicle. This means that it is a plane that flies without a pilot inside of it. Instead, a crew inside a ground station far away controls the Predator.

The Predator is used both as a spy plane and as a combat, or fighting, plane. In combat, the Predator can shoot missiles. When it is used as a spy plane, the Predator has cameras that send pictures to the plane's crew. These pictures can then be used to see where the enemy is.

**20** *This picture shows the Boeing Dreamliner being built at a Boeing factory in Everett, Washington.*

# Tomorrow's Planes

People are working hard to make planes better. Some people are even building planes that use less fuel. Fuel is what powers airplanes. Building and flying planes costs a lot of money. A plane that uses less fuel would be less costly to fly. Using less fuel would also be better for the **environment**.

The Boeing 787 Dreamliner is an example of a new environmentally friendly plane. The Dreamliner will use 20 percent less fuel than other planes its size, while still being one of the fastest commercial planes in the air. The amount of harmful gases that the Dreamliner puts out will also be 20 percent less than the amount other planes its size put out.

# Changing the World

Planes have changed the way people live. In the 1800s, people traveled for months to get from Missouri to California in horse-drawn wagons. Today, you can fly from Missouri to California in just a few hours! Airplanes, whether they are big or small, above the ground or above the water, are allowing people to travel with ease. Military planes are helping keep people safe. These super fast machines use speed and technology to do these things.

Airplanes will always be useful, and they keep getting faster and more environmentally friendly. We look forward to seeing what these excellent vehicles can do next!

# Glossary

**cargo** (KAHR-goh)  The load of goods carried by an airplane, a ship, or an automobile.

**commercial** (kuh-MER-shul)  Having to do with business or trade.

**composite** (kum-PO-zut)  Made up of many parts from different places.

**environment** (en-VY-ern-ment)  All the living things and conditions of a place.

**gliders** (GLY-derz)  Aircraft that fly without motors.

**gravity** (GRA-vih-tee)  The force that causes objects to move toward each other.

**materials** (muh-TEER-ee-ulz)  What something is made of.

**missiles** (MIH-sulz)  Weapons that are shot at something far away.

**passenger** (PA-sin-jur)  A person who rides in or on a moving thing.

**piloted** (PY-lut-ed)  Operated by a person.

**pressure** (PREH-shur)  A force that pushes on something.

**radar** (RAY-dar)  A machine that uses radio waves to find objects.

**supersonic** (soo-per-SAH-nik)  Moving faster than the speed of sound.

**weapons** (WEH-punz)  Objects used to hurt or kill.

# Index

# Web Sites

Due to the changing nature of Internet links, PowerKids Press has developed an online list of Web sites related to the subject of this book. This site is updated regularly. Please use this link to access the list:
www.powerkidslinks.com/stat/plane/